Bannockburn School Dist. 106
2165 Telegraph Road
Bannockburn, Illinois 60015

SIMPLY SCIENCE

Magnets

Bannockburn School Dist. 106
2165 Telegraph Road
Bannockburn, Illinois 60015

by Darlene R. Stille

Content Advisers: Terrence E. Young Jr., M.Ed., M.L.S.,
Jefferson Parish (La.) Public Schools, and Janann Jenner, Ph.D.

Reading Adviser: Dr. Linda D. Labbo,
Department of Reading Education, College of Education,
The University of Georgia

COMPASS POINT BOOKS

Minneapolis, Minnesota

Compass Point Books
3109 West 50th Street, #115
Minneapolis, MN 55410

Visit Compass Point Books on the Internet at *www.compasspointbooks.com* or e-mail your request to *custserv@compasspointbooks.com*

Editors: E. Russell Primm, Emily J. Dolbear, and Melissa Stewart
Photo Researcher: Svetlana Zhurkina
Photo Selector: Matthew Eisentrager-Warner
Designer: Bradfordesign, Inc.

Library of Congress Cataloging-in-Publication Data

Stille, Darlene R.
    Magnets / by Darlene Stille.
        p. cm. — (Simply science)
    Includes bibliographical references and index.
    ISBN 0-7565-0091-5 (hardcover : lib. bdg.)
    ISBN 0-7565-0972-6 (paperback)
        1. Magnetism—Juvenile literature. 2. Magnets—Juvenile literature. [1. Magnetism.
2. Magnets.] I. Title. II. Simply science (Minneapolis, Minn.)
    QC753.7 .S75 2001
    538—dc21   00-010942

Table of Contents

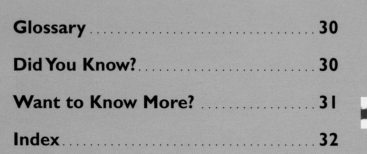

What Is a Magnet?

Look at your refrigerator. Do you see a magnet there? A magnet can stick to a refrigerator door all by itself. You do not need glue or tape to hold it there.

You cannot make a piece of cloth or a rubber ball stick to a refrigerator. They are not magnets.

◀ Magnets on a refrigerator

Magnets stick to metal ▶
but do not stick to cloth.

Glass, feathers, and wood are not magnets either. But some rocks can be magnets. A rock called **lodestone** is a magnet.

Some kinds of metal can be made into magnets too. Iron, nickel, and cobalt are metals that can become magnets.

Lodestone is a magnet.

Sometimes it can be hard to pull magnets apart. ▶

Magnets Push or Pull

It is fun to play with magnets. Some magnets are shaped like a "U." They are called horseshoe magnets. Bar magnets are long and straight.

All magnets can make things move without touching them. Nails and other pieces of metal will move toward a magnet.

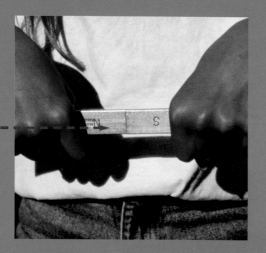

Magnets come in different shapes and sizes.

A magnet has two ends. Each end is called a **pole**. One pole is called the north pole. The other pole is called the south pole. Every magnet has a north pole and a south pole.

The north pole of one magnet pulls toward the south pole of another magnet. But the north poles of two magnets push away from each other. The south poles of two magnets also push away from each other.

The Force of Magnets

Hold a magnet far away from a refrigerator door. Then let go of the magnet. What happens? The magnet falls to the floor. Now hold the magnet closer to the refrigerator and see what happens. When the magnet is close enough, it will jump to the refrigerator door.

Magnets can repel each other. The force of these two magnets makes it look like one is floating in the air.

◀ The north and south poles of two magnets

Try the same thing with a bar magnet and some iron nails. Does the magnet move toward the nails? Why do you think this happens? It happens because there is an area around a magnet called a **magnetic field**.

A magnet can pull on objects inside its magnetic field. When you put an iron nail inside a bar magnet's magnetic field, the nail will jump to the magnet.

This magnet pulls iron filings to it or pushes them away.

A magnetic field goes out in half circles.

You cannot see a magnetic field. But you can imagine that it looks like lines. The lines start at one pole. They go out in a half circle from the magnet. The lines end at the other pole. A nail inside these lines will be pulled toward a bar magnet.

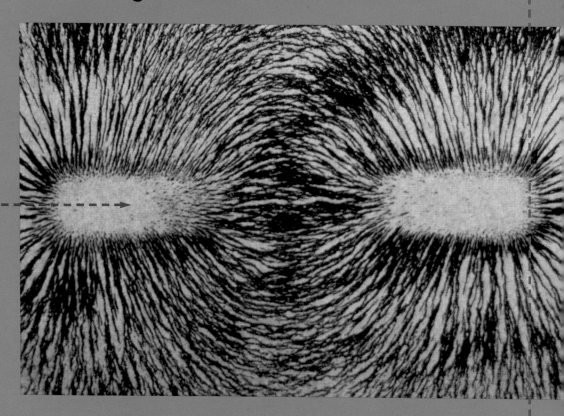

Big and Small Magnets

Magnets come in all sizes. Some magnets are as big as a house. They are powerful enough to lift a car. These magnets are used in junkyards and steel mills.

The earth itself is a giant magnet. The sun is an even bigger magnet.

A junkyard magnet   The sun

Earth and the sun have north and south poles.

Some **atoms** can be magnets. An atom is so tiny that you cannot see it. Millions of atoms would fit on the period at the end of this sentence. Everything in the world is made up of atoms.

A diagram of an atom ▶

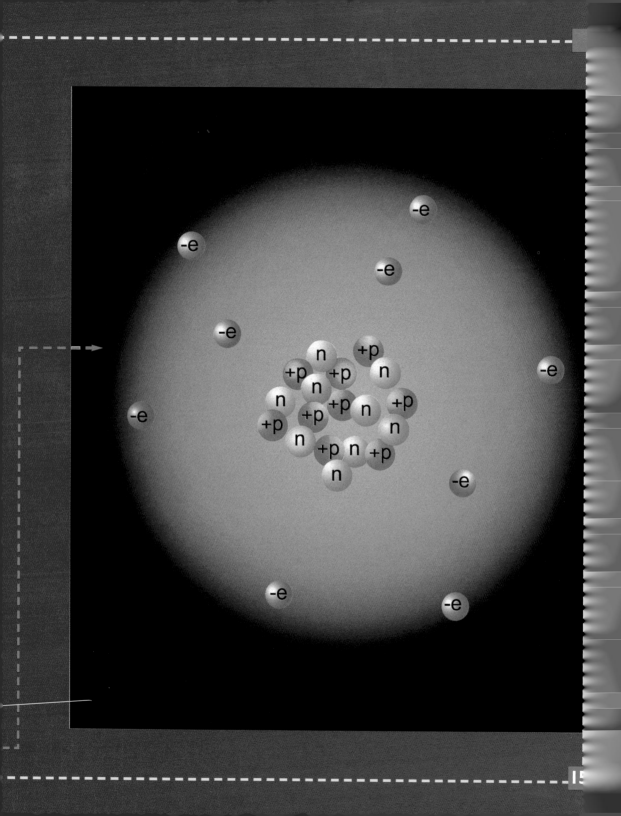

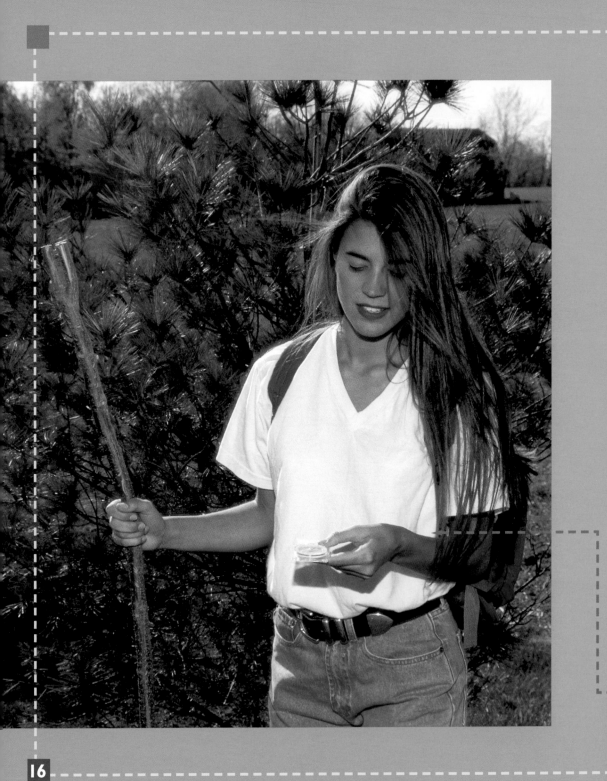

Making a Compass

Sailors have used **compasses** for hundreds of years. A compass can help people figure out where they are. It can also tell them where they are going. If you get lost in the woods, you can use a compass to help you find your way home. Every compass is made from a magnet.

Using a compass on a hike

Compasses help you with direction. ▶

To make your own compass, you will need a small bar magnet and a piece of string. Tie the string around the middle of the magnet. Now let the magnet hang from the string. The magnet will swing around and point in one direction.

A bar magnet tied to a string

Earth makes a compass point north.

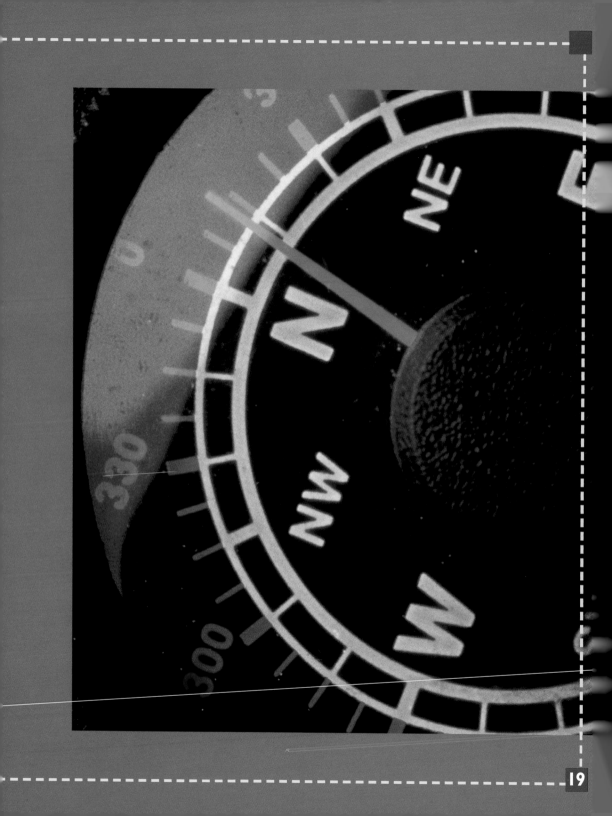

Even if you move or turn, the magnet will still point in the same direction. One end of the magnet will always point north. This happens because Earth is a giant magnet. Earth's powerful magnetic field makes the south pole of a bar magnet point north.

A compass always has a magnetic needle. The tip of the needle points north. A compass also has a card under the needle. The card shows the directions—east, west, north, and south. If a person wants to go west, you can use a compass to decide where to walk or how to steer your bike.

Magnets and Motors

People have known about magnets for a long time. They discovered magnetism after they learned to make iron tools. They saw that pieces of iron would stick to lodestone.

In the 1800s, scientists learned that magnets could be

People found that iron tools ▶ would stick to lodestone.

used to make **electric motors**.
Electric motors make things move.

An electric motor is made of wire
and magnets. The wire loops around
the magnets. The magnets and the
electric current in the wire make a
part in the motor move.
The moving part
makes the motor
work.

A small electric motor

The wires in a motor loop ▶
around the magnets.

You could not have electric fans without magnets. You could not have refrigerators, power drills, or vacuum cleaners without magnets. Without magnets, you could not have anything that runs on an electric motor.

◀ *An electric fan*

How We Use Magnets

You already know that we use magnets in electric motors, compasses, and refrigerators. We also use magnets in many other ways. A special kind of magnetic tape holds sound and pictures. That means you can watch movies on videotapes.

Videotapes store sound and pictures on a magnetic tape.

Magnets can also help us see inside the body. A special machine uses magnets to take pictures of the body. Taking this kind of picture is called **MRI** (Magnetic Resonance Imaging).

MRIs use magnets to take pictures of our bodies.

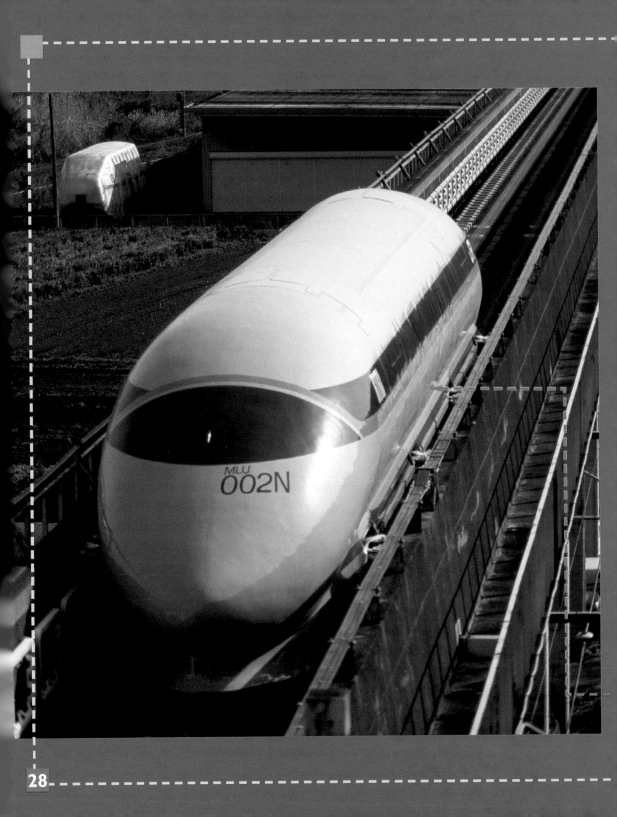

Magnets can even make special trains float in the air. They are called **maglev trains**. Remember how the north pole of one magnet pushes away from the north pole of another magnet? Powerful magnets in a maglev train push away from magnets in the track it runs on. This pushing force lifts the train up and lets it move without touching the track. It looks like magic. But it really is science.

◀ *A maglev train*

Glossary

atoms—tiny units of matter. Everything in the world is made of atoms.

compasses—instruments used to show direction and help people find their way

electric motors—machines that use magnets to make energy to run appliances and other equipment

magnetic field—the area around a magnet where its pulling power is felt

MRI (Magnetic Resonance Imaging)—a process used to help doctors see inside the body

Did You Know?

- Some small creatures have tiny lodestone crystals in their bodies. These crystals help guide them the same way that a compass helps a person.

- Earth has a stronger magnetic field than Venus, Mars, or Mercury.

- When particles from the sun come into contact with Earth's magnetic field, people in some parts of North America can see glowing red and green lights in the sky at night. These are called the Northern Lights.

Want to Know More?

At the Library

Branley, Franklin Mansfield. *What Makes a Magnet.* New York: HarperTrophy, 1996.

Herschell, Michael. *Magnet Magic.* New York: HarperCollins, 1998.

Riley, Peter. *Magnetism.* Danbury, Conn.: Franklin Watts, 1999.

On the Web

For more information on *magnets,* use FactHound

to track down Web sites related to this book.

1. Go to *www.facthound.com*

2. Type in a search word related to this

   book or this book ID: 0756500915.

3. Click on the *Fetch It* button.

Your trusty FactHound will fetch the best Web sites for you!

Through the Mail

Edmund Scientific

101 East Gloucester Pike

Barrington, NJ 08007

To order a variety of magnets and directions for a few fun experiments

On the Road

National High Magnetic Field Lab

1800 East Paul Dirac Drive

Tallahassee, FL 32310

850/644-031

To tour this national research center and see some of the largest magnets in the world

Index

About the Author

Darlene R. Stille is a science editor and writer. She has lived in Chicago, Illinois, all her life. When she was in high school, she fell in love with science. While attending the University of Illinois, she discovered that she also enjoyed writing. Today she feels fortunate to have a career that allows her to pursue both her interests. Darlene R. Stille has written more than thirty books for young people.